YOU'VE GOT WHAT THIS WORLD NEEDS

DO YOU REALIZE THE WONDER
YOU POSSESS? IT RADIATES
AND ENCIRCLES YOU.
IT'S IMPOSSIBLE TO MISS.

FROM THE GLIMMER IN YOUR EYES
TO THE POSSIBILITIES FILLING
YOUR POCKETS, IT'S CLEAR—
YOU'VE GOT WHAT THIS WORLD NEEDS.

YOUR MARVELS ARE TOO MANY
TO BE COUNTED, YOUR SPIRIT
TOO BRILLIANT TO GO UNNOTICED.

WITH ALL YOU HAVE NOW AND ALL YOU'RE BOUND TO ACCOMPLISH, ONE DAY YOU COULD LIGHT THE WHOLE DANG WORLD. (I KNOW, BECAUSE YOU ALREADY BRIGHTEN MINE.)

WHAT IF I TOLD YOU...
YOU DON'T NEED ONE MORE THING?

WHAT IF I SAID, THERE'S SIMPLY NOTHING
THAT COULD MAKE YOU COOLER,
MORE INSPIRING, OR MORE WORTHY
OF ADMIRATION THAN WHO
YOU ARE RIGHT NOW?

...BECAUSE YOU'VE GOT
EVERYTHING THAT COUNTS.

YOU HAVE THE RAW MATERIALS
FOR MAGIC, AND THE ESSENTIAL
INGREDIENTS FOR A
SPRINKLE-COATED LIFE.

YOU'RE OVERLOADED WITH GIFTS WORTH SHARING—PILES OF PRESENTS THAT MAKE ALL YOU TOUCH A LITTLE BETTER THAN BEFORE.

YOU HAVE BIG IDEAS AND
AN EVEN BIGGER HEART. YOUR SPARK
FLOATS THROUGH THE AIR AND IGNITES
SOMETHING REAL IN EVERYONE YOU MEET.

TO ME, YOU'RE LIKE AN EVERGREEN FOREST, AN OCEAN CURRENT, OR THE SUN ITSELF—SOMETHING MONUMENTAL, NECESSARY, AND TRUE.

AND HERE I AM, THE LUCKY ONE WHO GETS TO KNOW YOU.

DO YOU REALIZE THE IMPACT YOU HAVE?

DO YOU NOTICE THE WAVES YOU MAKE,
THE SURGE OF SPECTACULAR YOU UNLEASH
EACH DAY, AND THE REST OF US SURFERS
OUT HERE ENJOYING THE RIDE?

THE THING IS, THE WORLD
EVOLVES AND LOVE IS FOUND
THANKS TO THE VIBRANCY
AND BRAVERY OF PEOPLE
LIKE YOU.

YOU SHOW UP, YOU GIVE, YOU CREATE, YOU CONNECT, AND YOU BUILD—NOT BECAUSE IT LOOKS GOOD, BUT BECAUSE IT MATTERS SO MUCH, TO ME AND EVERYONE YOU KNOW.

JUST LOOK AT ALL YOU'VE ALREADY ACCOMPLISHED. STAND BACK AND WAVE TO THE MANY PEOPLE WHO COUNT YOU AMONG THEIR FRIENDS, THEIR CONFIDANTS, THEIR ALLIES, AND THEIR FAVORITES (LIKE ME! HI!).

WHEREVER YOU GO,
YOUR COLOR,
CONTRAST, AND POP
TURN EVERYDAY LIFE INTO
WALL-TO-WALL ART.

NOW THAT'S WHAT
I CALL SUCCESS.

WHAT IF I TOLD YOU THIS IS
JUST YOUR BEGINNING?

YOU'VE DONE SO MUCH GOOD,
AND THERE'S EVEN MORE
GREATNESS LEFT TO COME.

THERE'S NO MAP FOR THIS LIFE,
BUT YOU'VE GOT A COMPASS IN
YOUR HEART AND EVERYONE YOU
LOVE CHEERING YOU ON.

KEEP SHARING YOUR GIFTS
WITH THE WORLD. UNWRAP EACH ONE,
THROW IT INTO THE WIND,
AND LET IT FLY.

LET THE CHANGING OF
THE SEASONS BE YOUR MOOD BOARD,
AND THE FEELING OF A COZY ROOM
OVERFLOWING WITH FRIENDS,
YOUR NORTH STAR.

REMEMBER, THE BEST THINGS
IN LIFE ARE ALREADY YOURS.

...AND YOU'RE ONE OF
THE BEST THINGS IN MINE.

SO, TAKE A FEW CHANCES.
GIVE THE WORLD EVERYTHING
YOU'VE GOT.

...AND YOU'LL NEVER BE LOST.

COMPENDIUM®

live inspired

Written by: Danielle Leduc McQueen
Illustrated by: Marion Barraud
Edited by: Bailey Vega
Art Directed by: Jessica Phoenix

ISBN: 978-1-957891-58-3

1st printing. Printed in China with soy inks on FSC®-Mix certified paper.

Create meaningful moments with gifts that inspire.

CONNECT WITH US
live-inspired.com | sayhello@compendiuminc.com

@compendiumliveinspired
#compendiumliveinspired